WHO'S THE GOAT?
USING MATH TO CROWN THE CHAMPION™

CROSBY VS OVECHKIN VS McDAVID VS GRETZKY

I0808942

Jason Walker

rosen publishing's
rosen central®

New York

Published in 2020 by The Rosen Publishing Group, Inc.
29 East 21st Street, New York, NY 10010

First Edition

Library of Congress Cataloging-in-Publication Data

Names: Walker, Jason M., author.
Title: Crosby vs. Ovechkin vs. McDavid vs. Gretzky / Jason M. Walker.
Other titles: Crosby versus Ovechkin versus McDavid versus Gretzky
Description: New York : Rosen Central, 2020. | Series: Who's the GOAT? Using math to crown the champion | Includes bibliographical references and index. | Audience: Grade 5 to 8.
Identifiers: LCCN 2019004036| ISBN 9781725348448 (library bound) | ISBN 9781725348431 (pbk.)
Subjects: LCSH: Hockey players—Statistics—Juvenile literature. | Gretzky, Wayne, 1961– —Juvenile literature. | Ovechkin, Alexander, 1985– —Juvenile literature. | Crosby, Sidney, 1987– —Juvenile literature. | McDavid, Connor, 1997– —Juvenile literature. | Statistics—Juvenile literature. | Mathematics—Juvenile literature.
Classification: LCC GV848.5.A1 W35 2020 | DDC 796.9620922 [B]—dc23
LC record available at https://lccn.loc.gov/2019004036

Manufactured in the United States of America

CONTENTS

INTRODUCTION

Since the founding of the National Hockey League (NHL) in 1917, it has been the home of many of the most talented hockey players ever to touch the ice. As the league rose to prominence in the twentieth century—attracting elite skaters from Canada, the United States, and eventually Europe—it quickly became known as the premier ice hockey association in the world.

Throughout its storied history, great players have contributed to the development of not only the league, but the sport of hockey itself. Gordie Howe blazed the trail in the 1950s and 1960s, setting nearly every scoring record at the time, popularizing the sport, and earning the nickname "Mr. Hockey." In the 1960s and 1970s, Bobby Orr redefined what it was to be a defenseman, contributing to offensive rushes and becoming the only defensive player in history to lead the league in scoring. Many NHL legends have come and gone, each leaving a tangible mark on the game—and, perhaps more important, inspiring the next generation of players.

Wayne Gretzky, Alexander Ovechkin, Sidney Crosby, and Connor McDavid—four of the greatest skaters of all time—have each left their signature in the record books and in the annals of NHL history. Whether it is the record-setting story of Wayne Gretzky, the legendary

The logo of the National Hockey League—which is home to the most talented hockey players in the world—is shown here.

goal scoring of Alexander Ovechkin, the championship trophies of Sidney Crosby, or the limitless potential of Connor McDavid, each has excelled at the game in his own way.

Who is the greatest NHL player ever to lace up skates? The question has been around since the league was founded, and hockey fans have made the case for different superstars over the years. Oftentimes, the discussion of greatness involves statistics: who scored the most goals? Who won the most championships? Who got the most awards? In hockey, as in all sports, greatness is tied to statistics. In this book, mathematics and statistics will be used as a means of exploring this question.

To understand the discussions of the greatest of all time (GOAT), it is important to review common hockey terminology used for scorekeeping, which will be referenced repeatedly: goals, assists, and points. How well a player does on the ice is typically reflected by the number of goals, assists, and points that player scores. While they are not the only measurement of a player's greatness, they are typically the first consideration when analyzing NHL playmakers.

- **Goal:** when a player shoots the puck into the opposing team's net; worth one point.
- **Assist:** when a player aids another player who then scores a goal, typically by passing that player the puck shortly before a goal is scored; worth one point.
- **Point:** a symbolic representation of a goal or an assist; used to determine the number of goals and assists tallied by a player. As an equation, goals + assists = points. In hockey, both a goal and an assist are worth one point. For example, if a player scores one goal and two assists in a game, he or she has scored three points.

All statistics and award information is taken from NHL.com unless otherwise noted.

CHAPTER 1

WAYNE GRETZKY: THE GREAT ONE

Wayne Gretzky has left behind the greatest legacy in hockey history. It is arguable that no other athlete, from any sport, had a more impressive career. In his prime, Gretzky dominated the game in a way never before seen in professional North American sports. From record books to headlines, the shadow of Gretzky has loomed large over the game of hockey since he hung up his skates in 1999. It was well before that, though, when he attained the nickname he holds today: "the Great One."

HUMBLE BEGINNINGS

Born in Brantford, Ontario, Canada, in 1961, Wayne Gretzky spent his early years skating on his father's homemade ice rink in the backyard. It was said that Gretzky would spend almost all day, every day, practicing under his father's supervision, taking breaks only at mealtimes (and even then, he wore his skates). Gretzky would later attribute much of his famously creative style of play to his father's backyard training.

From an early age, it was apparent that Gretzky was a highly gifted hockey player. By the age of six, he had joined the local youth hockey program in Brantford, which was primarily comprised of ten-year-olds. Though he experienced growing pains his first few seasons, he eventually began to flourish, scoring a stunning 378 goals in one season in the minors. Soon, he became a rising star in Ontario and moved to Toronto to continue his youth career. Fourteen-year-old Gretzky recorded 60 points in twenty-eight games, competing against players four to six years his senior. It was not long before Gretzky became one of the premier youth hockey prospects in the world.

A young Gretzky, known then as the "White Tornado," is shown here posing for a youth skater photo in 1974.

RISE TO STARDOM

During his rookie professional season in the World Hockey Association (a lesser pro hockey league at the time), Gretzky was traded to the Edmonton Oilers and debuted as a centerman in

HOCKEY PLAYER, CRIME FIGHTER

As the biggest name in hockey, Gretzky was featured in many advertisements and products, perhaps none as bizarre as the short-lived 1991 animated children's show *Pro Stars*. Featuring an animated version of Gretzky, basketball player Michael Jordan, and football and baseball star Bo Jackson as a trio of crime fighters, the "Pro Bros" fought together to ward off evil and defeat supervillains. The associated *Pro Stars* cereal—whose box featured a picture of Gretzky in full hockey uniform—is still frequently bought and sold as a collectible item.

The *Pro Stars* poster shown here displays the trio of athletes featured on the program, including a helmetless Gretzky.

the NHL in 1979. While many doubted his ability to play successfully in the NHL, Gretzky outperformed his critics once again, scoring 137 points and tying for first in league scoring during his inaugural season. The following year, he would break the single-season point record, with 164, then proceed to break his own record shortly after, with 212. In that season, he would shatter Phil Esposito's single-season goals record of 76 with an unbelievable 92 goals—a record that still stands in 2019. With Gretzky rewriting the record books after only his third season in the NHL, it was apparent that the rise of the Great One had only just begun.

In the nine years Gretzky spent with the Oilers, an NHL dynasty was formed. On a team that included many future hall-of-famers, Gretzky and the Oilers quickly climbed their way to top. By the 1983–1984 season, they had clinched their first Stanley Cup, awarded to the NHL team that wins the league's championship series. During his tenure with the team, he would also capture the Hart Memorial Trophy—awarded to most valuable player (MVP) in the league—eight consecutive times. The team would emerge as Stanley Cup champions three more times before the magic finally came to an end in Edmonton.

END OF AN ERA

In one of the most shocking decisions ever made in professional sports, the Oilers traded Gretzky to the Los Angeles Kings in 1988. Being on a new team did not stop him from scoring at an unbelievable pace, and in 1989, he broke the NHL all-time points record of 1,850—held by Gordie Howe, his lifelong idol and childhood inspiration—at only twenty-eight years old. By the time he retired in 1999, he had exceeded Howe's legendary total by more than 1,000 points.

Wayne Gretzky's storied career ended in fitting fashion: while most players must wait three years after retirement to be eligible for the Hockey Hall of Fame, Gretzky was immediately inducted. For especially prominent, successful, and meaningful players, individual teams will at times "retire" the jersey number worn by that player, meaning no skater on that team can ever wear that number again. Gretzky's iconic jersey number—99—was retired league-wide by the NHL, an honor never bestowed before or after. Later, his first skates—a small, battered pair of blades that matched the homemade feel of his father's rink—would be displayed in the Hall of Fame, a tribute to the humble beginnings of a hopeful child who rose to be known as the Great One.

Stats at a Glance

Seasons	Games	Points	Points per game	Goals	Goals per game	Assists	Assists per game
20	1,487	2,857	1.92	894	0.60	1,963	1.32

WRITING THE BOOK

In many ways, the NHL record book reads like the personal memoirs of Wayne Gretzky. He is the owner of almost every premier career statistic, including total goals (894), assists (1,963), and points (2,857). When

Gretzky takes the ice as an Edmonton Oiler during the team's brief stint in the ill-fated World Hockey Association.

compared statistically to his peers, Gretzky crushes the competition. His assist total alone is greater than any other player's career point total—meaning that even if he had never scored a single goal in the NHL, he would still have more points than anyone else. Further, Gretzky played twenty seasons in the NHL; if he had retired after just his eleventh season, he would still have scored more points than any other player in history.

His statistical dominance also extends to single-season achievements, as he holds the record for most goals (92), assists (163), and points (215) in a single season. The 200-point season mark, once thought to be unachievable, was reached by Gretzky four times—a feat no other player has accomplished even once. Before Gretzky's career began, Phil Esposito held the record for most points in one season at 152. Gretzky would surpass this mark nine times. Similarly, the record for assists in a season before Gretzky belonged to Bobby Orr at 102—a total Gretzky would equal or surpass eleven times.

Fittingly, Gretzky is also the NHL leader in career points per game (1.92) and career assists per game (1.32). He sits at seventh all-time in career goals per game (0.60). To calculate points per game average, or PPG, divide the number of points he totaled throughout his career (2,857) by the number of games he played (1,487). The method is the same for goals and assists per game:

2,857 points ÷ 1,487 games = 1.92 PPG
894 goals ÷ 1,487 games = 0.60 GPG
1,963 assists ÷ 1,487 games = 1.32 APG

To put these numbers into perspective, only one other player in NHL history has averaged 1.5 PPG or above, and only one other averaged 1.0 APG or above. Gretzky cleared these benchmarks with ease.

COMPARING THE GREATS: GRETZKY VS. MCDAVID

How do Gretzky's numbers compare to modern-day stars? After leading the NHL in scoring two of his first three seasons, Connor McDavid is considered the best hockey player in the league today. Following a 108-point campaign in the 2017–2018 season, his career point total went up to 256. McDavid is scoring points at the highest rate in the game, but how long would it take him to equal Gretzky's legendary point total, assuming he maintained this pace?

First, calculate the difference between Gretzky's and McDavid's point totals. Gretzky scored 894 goals and 1,963 assists:

894 goals + 1,963 assists = 2,857 points

McDavid has scored 87 goals and 169 assists:

87 goals + 169 assists = 256 points

To find the difference, subtract the smaller total, 256, from the larger, 2,857:

2,857 points – 256 points = 2,601 points

This represents the number of points McDavid needs to equal Gretzky's. Next, calculate McDavid's PPG during his best statistical season. He notched 108 points in 2017–2018. He played in every game of the eighty-two-game season:

108 points ÷ 82 games = 1.32 PPG

The number of games required to equal Gretzky's record is unknown, so it will be represented by x. One season is made up of 82 games, so 82x represents the number of seasons needed to match the record. Multiply the unknown number of seasons—82x—by McDavid's best seasonal PPG—1.32—and set it equal to the difference in the two players' point totals:

The 2000 All-Star team is shown here watching as Gretzky's iconic jersey number of 99 is retired by the NHL.

$$1.32\ (82x) = 2{,}601$$
$$(1.32\ (82x)) \div 1.32 = 2{,}601 \div 1.32$$
$$82x = 1{,}970.45$$
$$82x \div 82 = 1{,}970.45 \div 82$$
$$x = 24.03 \text{ seasons}$$

Following this sequence of calculations, if Connor McDavid continued scoring at the league-leading pace he did in 2017–2018, it would take him approximately twenty-four more seasons—without missing a single game or slowing his rate down—to catch Wayne Gretzky's career point total. No small feat, especially since the average length of an NHL player's career is just 5.5 years, according to Bleacher Report.

In the modern NHL, due in part to evolving play styles and increased levels of competition in the league, most of Gretzky's records are considered unbreakable. If anyone does manage to break them, that player will not be wearing historic jersey number 99. That number, like many of those written in stone in the NHL record books, belongs solely to the Great One.

CHAPTER 2

ALEXANDER OVECHKIN: THE GREAT EIGHT

Russian-born Alexander Ovechkin, left winger for the Washington Capitals, is widely considered one of the NHL's most prolific goal scorers of all time. In the thirteen years since Ovechkin debuted in 2005, no other player has put the puck in the net more than "the Great Eight."

YOUTH ON ICE

Alexander Ovechkin was born in the Russian capital of Moscow during the days of the former Soviet Union. The son of two athletes, his athletic talent was obvious from an early age. Alexander was raised in a poor neighborhood and his parents spent the majority of their time working, but his athletic training was considered a top priority. His brother, Sergei, ensured he arrived at his training sessions and games. Alexander was ten years old when Sergei died in an unfortunate accident, and thereafter he dedicated his training and ongoing athletic success to his lost brother. After dominating in the Russian junior leagues, he became the most coveted hockey prospect in the upcoming 2004 NHL draft.

Even during his childhood in Russia, Ovechkin dreamed of playing in the NHL. In 2004, with the first overall selection in the NHL draft, the Washington Capitals made that dream a reality. Unfortunately, a dispute between the league and the NHL Players' Association caused the entire 2004–2005 NHL season to be lost, so he debuted in the 2005–2006 season along with another top prospect, Sidney Crosby. Since being drafted, Ovechkin has been the flagship of the Capitals franchise, going by the nicknames "Ovi" and the Great Eight—the latter inspired by his iconic jersey number, 8.

A young Ovechkin smiles after getting selected first overall in the 2004 NHL draft, kicking off his incredible career.

A QUICK TRANSITION

Ovechkin exploded out of the gate during his rookie season, scoring 106 points and capturing the Calder Memorial Trophy, which is awarded each season to the player voted as the most outstanding rookie.

His performance quickly fueled a turnaround for the struggling Washington franchise, with the Capitals making the playoffs ten of the next thirteen seasons. He eventually evolved into a respected veteran presence in the Washington locker room, earning the title of team captain in 2010, which he has held ever since.

Ovechkin is shown here posing after winning the 2006 Calder Memorial Trophy for most outstanding rookie.

Ovechkin had his greatest statistical season in 2007–2008 when he notched 47 assists and a career-high 65 goals, making him the only player to score more than 60 goals in a season in the current millennium. His heroics earned him distinction as the MVP, top goal scorer, top point scorer, and winner of the Ted Lindsay Award. This award is an NHL Players' Association accolade granted to the most outstanding player in a season. This remarkable achievement made him the first NHL player in history to secure all four awards in one season.

TRIBUTE TO FAMILY

Ovechkin often points to the sky after scoring in remembrance of his brother.

Though Ovechkin's athletic talents are truly spectacular, he attributes much of his success to his family and honors them in various ways on the ice. His jersey number, 8, was the number his mother wore while playing professional basketball. After scoring a goal, Ovi will often kiss his glove and point to the sky, a tribute to his late brother, Sergei—a name his son also bears. He has never forgotten the strong family support system that helped him become a junior—and now internationally acclaimed professional—superstar.

WINNING IT ALL

While Ovi's elite playmaking ability has made the postseason a regular occurrence for the high-flying Capitals, the ultimate honor of a Stanley Cup victory eluded Ovechkin for almost his entire career. That finally changed in the 2017–2018 season, as the Ovechkin-led Capitals defeated the Las Vegas Golden Knights to seize the franchise's first-ever Stanley Cup championship. The championship was the final measure of success for a boy who grew up hoarding hockey cards in his room in Moscow, dreaming of one day playing in a faraway land. After years of hard work, intense training, and frequent heartbreaks, he was finally a world champion at the pinnacle of his sport.

Stats at a Glance

Seasons	Games	Points	Points per game	Goals	Goals per game	Assists	Assists per game
13	1,003	1,122	1.12	607	0.61	515	0.51

LIGHTING THE LAMP

While Ovechkin's overall statistics are already comparable to many NHL legends, he has always been a goal scorer first and foremost. His goal total of 607 is the most for any active player following the 2017–2018 season. His 0.61 goals per game (GPG) average sits at sixth best in NHL history, ranking him ahead of even Gretzky. To calculate his GPG, take the number of goals he has scored (607) and divide it by the number of games he has played (1,003); the quotient will be his GPG: 607 goals ÷ 1,003 games = 0.61 GPG. In comparison, Gretzky scored 894 goals in 1,487 games: 894 goals ÷ 1,487 games = 0.60 GPG.

Because multiple assists are often awarded for each goal in hockey, a player's assists typically overtake goals scored. Ovechkin is one of only eight players in NHL history to have more than 1,000 points while having more goals than assists, and he is the only player whose professional career is in the twenty-first century.

The Maurice "Rocket" Richard Trophy, given yearly to the player who scores the most goals in the regular season, has been presented to Ovi seven times, tying him with the legendary Bobby Hull for the number of times he has led the league in goal scoring.

COMPARING THE GREATS: OVI VS. GRETZKY, CROSBY, AND McDAVID

It is no surprise that to score, a player has to shoot. While some players are more reserved, Ovechkin is well known for letting the puck rip. His 2018 shot total of 4,896 is already eighth all time. How many shots per game does this equate to, and how does this compare to other greats? To calculate shots per game, divide his shot total (4,896) by the number of games he has played (1,003). Doing the same calculation with the other three players featured here, the results are:

- Ovechkin: 4,896 shots ÷ 1,003 games = 4.88 shots per game
- Gretzky: 5,088 shots ÷ 1,487 games = 3.42 shots per game
- Crosby: 2,843 shots ÷ 864 games = 3.29 shots per game
- McDavid: 630 shots ÷ 209 games = 3.01 shots per game

Every hockey player dreams of winning the Stanley Cup, and Ovi finally got to realize that dream in 2018, after years of impressive individual play.

Clearly, no other great shoots more than Ovechkin. To put the shot numbers in another perspective, it is possible to calculate the percentage of shots a player contributes to his team's shot total. In other words: for every 100 shots the Washington Capitals take, how many belong to Ovechkin, on average? This is calculated by dividing his shot total (4,896) by the total number of shots taken by the team since he was drafted (31,145). To translate the result to a percentage, move the decimal place to the right twice. Repeating this process for each skater, the results are:

- Ovechkin: 4,896 shots ÷ 31,145 team shots = 0.16 (16 percent)
- Gretzky: 5,088 shots ÷ 48,799 team shots = 0.10 (10 percent)
- Crosby: 2,843 shots ÷ 32,138 team shots = 0.09 (9 percent)
- McDavid: 630 shots ÷ 7,673 team shots = 0.08 (8 percent)

Once again, Ovi dominates, contributing a much greater percentage of shots to his team than anyone else. Accordingly, his goals and goals per game are equally impressive.

RACE FOR THE RECORD

Gretzky Goals	Ovechkin Goals	Goals Needed	Ovechkin GPG	Estimated Games Needed	Estimated Seasons Needed
894	607	287	0.61	470.49	5.74

With Ovechkin scoring goals at breakneck pace, he is one of the few players with a realistic chance to break Gretzky's career goals record of 894. In the top twenty for career goals at the age of thirty-three, Ovechkin is primed to continue his climb upward as he chases the title. Can he break one of the most coveted records in all of hockey? It depends on whether Ovechkin can continue his career goal-scoring pace and for how long.

Using Ovi's statistics, it is possible to estimate how long the race might take.

First, it is necessary to find how many goals he will need to equal the record. Subtract Ovechkin's number of goals (607) from Gretzky's number of goals (894):

894 goals – 607 goals = 287 goals

This represents the number of goals Ovi will have to score to reach Gretzky. The number of games needed by Ovi to reach Gretzky is unknown, so it will be represented by x. However, it is known that he must score 287 goals to equal the record. Therefore, the product of his goals per game (0.61) and the unknown number of games he must play to score those goals (x) must equal the 287 goals needed. Translate this to a mathematical equation, then solve for x:

$0.61x = 287$
$0.61x \div 0.61 = 287 \div 0.61$
$x = 470.49$ games

According to these calculations, Ovi must play 470.49 games (while scoring an average of 0.61 goals per game) to score 287 goals, which is the difference between his career goal total and Gretzky's. Further, as there are eighty-two games in an NHL season, dividing this total by eighty-two results in the estimated number of seasons the race would take: 470.49 games ÷ 82 games per season = 5.74 seasons.

This means that Ovechkin would have to play until he is about forty years old. With some players in the modern era surpassing that age, it does not seem out of the question for the Great Eight to cement himself as one of the greatest by overtaking the original Great One's goals record.

CHAPTER 3

SIDNEY CROSBY: THE NEXT ONE

Since the generation-defining greatness of Wayne Gretzky, hockey fans, coaches, and sportwriters have always been on the search for the next great NHL player. In the 1980s, the NHL was the story of the Great One. In the 2000s, the story turned a new chapter, as Sidney Crosby rose from child prodigy to be known as "the Next One."

SID THE KID

Sidney Crosby was born in Nova Scotia, Canada, in the late 1980s. The young Sidney always excelled against his competition, and he was allowed to play at the midget youth level (typically reserved for ages fifteen to seventeen) by age fourteen. In his first season as a midget, he produced 217 points. Crosby's reputation exploded, earning him national press coverage in Canada and his lingering nicknames, "Sid the Kid" and the Next One. His dominance of youth hockey would continue throughout the juniors, and well before his

NHL draft availability, he was at the top of every team's prospect board.

Crosby's transition into the NHL was slightly unorthodox. In most NHL seasons, draft order is produced by a lottery system that is weighted so that only the worst teams have a realistic chance of grabbing the first draft pick. However, after an NHL Players' Association lockout resulted in the cancellation of the entire 2004–2005 NHL season, there were no standings to rely on, and the draft lottery was much more random. Due to Crosby's popularity as an elite, game-changing prospect, the draft was nicknamed the Sidney Crosby Sweepstakes. When the first lottery ball was drawn, it displayed the logo for the Pittsburgh Penguins—and Crosby has defined that franchise ever since.

A HEAD START

Crosby wasted no time establishing himself among the elite. In his rookie year in the NHL, his 63 assists and 102 points broke Penguins' rookie records set by the all-time great Mario Lemieux. After his 120-point sophomore season, he became the youngest Art Ross Trophy winner—granted to the player who scores the most points throughout the regular season—as well as the youngest Ted Lindsay Award winner. Further, each year, the NHL hosts an All-Star Game in which the best in the league are voted onto one ultimate roster. After

LUCKY NUMBER 87

Crosby's jersey number, 87, reflects the date of his birth: August 7, 1987, or 8/7/87. Further, after Crosby's initial three-year rookie deal ended, he signed a five-year, $43.5 million contract—earning him an average of $8.7 million per year. His contract in 2012—a twelve-year, $104.4 million extension—also pays him an average of $8.7 million per year. It is believed that the number 87 holds superstitious value to him, though according to Penguins general manager Ray Shero, he declined the option to earn more money because he wanted to help the team financially.

Just as with Gretzky's 99 and Ovechkin's 8, Crosby's 87 has become an icon for hockey fans everywhere.

his 2006–2007 season, Crosby became the youngest player ever voted to an All-Star Game roster. Shortly after, he became the youngest team captain in NHL history at the time.

FACE OF THE LEAGUE

It was not long before Crosby's ascent catapulted the Penguins to postseason success. His addition to the team propelled Pittsburgh into the playoffs twelve of

Led by Crosby's elite playmaking ability, the Penguins are frequent participants in the postseason.

the thirteen seasons since he entered the league. In 2008–2009, Crosby notched 103 points and led the Penguins to their first Stanley Cup victory since 1992. Following a few injury-plagued seasons, Crosby helped Pittsburgh to another championship victory in 2015–2016, then another the following year, making the Penguins the first back-to-back Stanley Cup winners in nearly twenty years. Along the way, Crosby would grab another point-scoring title, two goal-scoring titles, and two MVP awards.

For more than a decade, Sidney Crosby has been the face of the NHL. As an All-Star, record setter, and Stanley Cup champion, the Nova Scotian has become a household name in North American sports. Crosby has become a generation-defining player, representing the pinnacle of the sport for a long time, just like the Great One before him. Astoundingly, he has lived up to the label bestowed on him at a young age, and through blood, sweat, and championships, became the Next One.

Stats at a Glance

Seasons	Games	Points	Points per game	Goals	Goals per game	Assists	Assists per game
13	864	1,116	1.29	411	0.48	705	0.82

A Career of Greatness

With plenty of hockey still ahead of him, Crosby's career statistics are striking. Among active players who started their NHL careers in the twenty-first century, Crosby has the second-most points, second-most goals, and the most assists.

Due in large part to his team's success, he is also one of the most prolific playoff scorers of all time. Despite Ovechkin's undeniable knack for the net, Crosby has scored 5 more playoff goals than Ovi, for a total of 66. His 119 playoff assists are the twelfth most all time, and his playoff point total of 185 ranks him at tenth all time. He will likely only continue to climb the record books of postseason glory as his career continues.

COMPARING THE GREATS: SID VS. OVI

While Crosby's totals are impressive, his per-game averages are his most elite stats. Due to several injuries throughout his career, Crosby played just one full 82-game season between 2005 and 2018. As such, he has logged fewer games than many of his colleagues in his era, including Ovechkin. Ovi has played a total of 1,003 games as of the 2017–2018 season, 139 more than Crosby: 1,003 games – 864 games = 139 games.

Despite this fact, Ovechkin has just six more career points than Crosby. It is easy to see, before any further calculation, that Crosby scores more points on average. The professional and statistical rivalry between these two giants has helped define the NHL since they were drafted, so many have wondered what Crosby's stats would be like if he had not missed so much playing time.

First, calculate each player's PPG. To find this average, take the total number of points Crosby has earned (1,116) and divide it by the number of games he has played (864). Repeating the same operation for his goals and assists, the results are:

1,116 points ÷ 864 games = 1.29 PPG
411 goals ÷ 864 games = 0.48 GPG
705 assists ÷ 864 games = 0.82 APG

These numbers represent the average number of points, goals, and assists he has scored in each game of his career. These averages rank him sixth all time for career PPG and fifth all time for career APG. The same operations can be done to calculate Ovechkin's averages:

1,122 points ÷ 1,003 games = 1.12 PPG
607 goals ÷ 1,003 games = 0.61 GPG
515 assists ÷ 1,003 games = 0.51 APG

Now that the averages have been found, Crosby's hypothetical points over Ovechkin's number of games played (1,003) can be calculated. To achieve this, take his PPG (1.29), and multiply it by Ovechkin's number of games played: 1.29 PPG × 1,003 games = 1,294 points. The difference between Ovechkin's point total over that time (1,122) is: 1,294 points – 1,122 points = 172 points.

According to these calculations, if Sidney Crosby had played the same number of games as Alexander Ovechkin, he hypothetically would have put up 172 more points—a considerable number, considering his competition.

SNIPER

Putting the puck in the net is the ultimate goal, but not all shots are created equal. Elite players in the NHL know when to shoot and where to put the puck when

Crosby has a knack for putting the puck in the net, as he is shown here doing it against the Ottawa Senators in the playoffs.

they do. Scoring proficiency per shot can be represented statistically by a player's shooting percentage, which demonstrates how often shots actually result in goals. Sidney Crosby is one of the best in the league when it comes to accuracy—and he has the math to back it up.

A player's shooting percentage is calculated by taking his total goals and dividing it by his total number of shots—this will result in the percentage of shots that resulted in goals. Finding Crosby's shooting percentage is similar to answering an important question: out of 100 shots, how many goals does Sidney Crosby score on average? As of the 2017–2018 season, he has 411 goals in his career on 2,843 shots. In dividing his goals by his shots and comparing with the other greats, the results are:

- Gretzky: 894 goals ÷ 5,088 shots = 0.1757 (17.57 percent)
- Crosby: 411 goals ÷ 2,843 shots = 0.1446 (14.46 percent)
- McDavid: 256 shots ÷ 630 shots = 0.1381 (13.81 percent)
- Ovechkin: 607 goals ÷ 4,896 shots = 0.1240 (12.40 percent)

At first glance, it may appear as though Wayne Gretzky dominates in this area, as his shooting percentage is considerably higher than the others. However, Gretzky also played in an era when shooting percentages overall were higher than they are today. Crosby's 14.46 percent shooting percentage lands him in the top ten for active players as of the 2017–2018 season, and second for players with at least 1,500 shots in their careers.

If Sidney Crosby retired following the 2017–2018 season, he would unquestionably find himself in the Hall of Fame. However, at just thirty-one years old, the only question remaining for the Next One is how many more Stanley Cup trophies he will bring home before he hangs up his skates.

CHAPTER 4

CONNOR McDAVID: THE NEW NHL

While other all-time great hockey players have written most of their stories already, Connor McDavid has only just begun. Wayne Gretzy played for twenty years; Crosby and Ovechkin may each match or exceed that total. Even after just a few seasons in the NHL, McDavid has already established himself among the elite. Much like Gretzky was the face of hockey during his time, and Crosby and Ovechkin were in their primes, many believe that Connor McDavid is destined to become the face of the NHL in the late 2010s, 2020s, and beyond.

WONDER KID

Born in 1997 in a suburb of Toronto, Connor McDavid's childhood was similar to those of stars of previous generations. At age three, he was roller-skating in his family's basement and practicing his slap shot. Like Gretzky, Connor's father supervised and guided his development from the beginning, designing obstacle courses for his young son to practice his stickhandling.

After impressing scouts in his youth hockey programs, he was one of the hottest prospects for the Ontario Hockey League (OHL), one of the major junior hockey leagues in Canada. His skill level was considered to be

A young McDavid is shown here celebrating after a goal during the 2014 World Junior Ice Hockey Championships.

so great that he was permitted to enter the OHL a year earlier than the age minimum, an honor given previously only to John Tavares and Aaron Ekblad—both of whom later became NHL stars. After years of dominating the OHL, he was atop every NHL draft board and the envy of every general manager in the league. McDavid was the next big thing in hockey, before he was even wearing an NHL jersey.

SKATE TO THE TOP

In the 2015 NHL draft, the Edmonton Oilers selected McDavid with the first overall pick. Much like Sidney Crosby ten years prior, he was considered the obvious choice—a generational talent who would be able to put a franchise on his back and pull them to a championship. Much like Crosby, McDavid's skills did not disappoint.

Since joining the league, McDavid's performance has been nothing short of spectacular. Despite an injury-plagued rookie season, he averaged more than one point per game (16 goals + 32 assists = 48 points; 48 points ÷ 45 games = 1.06 points per game) and was named captain of the Oilers after the season. His second year, he recorded 30 goals and 70 assists for a total of 100 points, enough to secure the Art Ross Trophy. In the 2017–2018 season, he kept the Art Ross Trophy for another year, notching 41 goals and 67 assists for a league-leading 108 points. In doing so, he would

PASSING THE TORCH

Like most young hockey fans, McDavid was enamored with the NHL elite, including his favorite player: Sidney Crosby. At fifteen years old, McDavid made and presented a video biography of the Penguins star for a high school class. Just five years later, McDavid would put up more points than Sidney Crosby in the NHL while capturing his first Art Ross Trophy. Following that season, he would be named captain of the Oilers, becoming the youngest team captain in NHL history—a distinction previously held by Crosby. In 2018, Crosby himself would declare McDavid the best player in the league during an interview with NHL.com.

The late 2010s were an incredible time to be a hockey fan; all-time greats and rising stars alike were playing against each other, such as Crosby against McDavid, shown here.

become the first back-to-back season points leader in seventeen years.

Even the best players, however, cannot do it on their own. Despite McDavid's unbelievable playmaking, the Oilers have not had the team success enjoyed by other greats. No one doubts that McDavid—the new face of the NHL—has the talent to win a championship. Once the pieces fall into place in Edmonton, it is only a matter of when that title victory will occur.

Seasons	Games	Points	Points per game	Goals	Goals per game	Assists	Assists per game
3	209	256	1.22	87	0.42	169	0.81

THE ART ROSS RACE

Compared to other GOAT candidates, McDavid's career totals may appear modest. However, he is only a few years into what will likely to be a long, productive career in the NHL, so it would be unfair to contrast his totals to those who have played for more than a decade. In comparing his per-game averages, his excellence is more accurately seen.

One of the most impressive feats McDavid has accomplished so far is leading the league in points in two of his first three seasons. The Art Ross Trophy, awarded to each season's point leader, is a time-honored and prestigious NHL award. Unsurprisingly, Wayne Gretzky has the most career Art Ross Trophies, with ten. However, McDavid has captured the award twice already, making it possible that he has a realistic shot of taking that record. How many points would he need to score per season to make this a reality?

To find out, a sample of point leaders will be needed. To keep things relevant to modern times, the sample of point leaders will be the ten trophy winners from the 2008–2009 season to the 2017–2018 season. From there, a mean, median, and mode can be found, each of which grant a different perspective of how many points may be required. The following list is the number of points each of the past ten Art Ross Trophy winners recorded:

108, 100, 106, 87, 104, 60, 109, 104, 112, 113

The mean, or average, of a set of numbers is the most common way to demonstrate a statistical average. To find the mean, add the numbers in the list and divide by the number of summed numbers:

$$108 + 100 + 106 + 87 + 104 + 60 + 109 + 104 + 112 + 113 = 1{,}003$$
$$1003 \div 10 = 100.3$$

The median of a set of numbers represents the middlemost value, when all numbers are listed from least to greatest. In an odd-numbered list, there will always be one number in the middle; however, for an even-numbered list, there will be two. In this case, find the average of the middle two numbers to obtain the median:

60, 87, 100, 104, 104, 106, 108, 109, 112, 113

Middle values: 104, 106.

104 + 106 = 210
210 ÷ 2 = 105

The mode of a set of numbers is simply the number that occurs most in that list, if any. This is most easily done after sorting the list from least to greatest, similar to finding the median:

60, 87, 100, 104, 104, 106, 108, 109, 112, 113

As 104 is the only number to occur multiple times in the list, it is the mode of this set of numbers.

The mean of 100.3, median of 105, and mode of 104 represent three different ways to view the number of points needed to win an Art Ross Trophy in modern times. In the first two seasons McDavid played in a full 82 games, he scored 100 and 108 points. His average, therefore, can be calculated:

100 + 108 = 208

$208 \div 2 = 104$

The average number of points he has scored in a full season is 104. This total surpasses the mean of 100.3 and the mode of 104, but falls slightly short of the median of 105. If McDavid keeps this performance up, it is realistic to estimate that his point totals will put him within reach of the Art Ross Trophy every season, regardless of what "average" is used to estimate the winner.

COMPARING THE GREATS: McDAVID VS. CROSBY AND OVI

McDavid's averages are on par with other greats, so what could McDavid's statistics be like by the time he has played for as long as Crosby and Ovechkin? To help estimate this, first find the average number of games played by these two stars across thirteen seasons. Crosby has played 894; Ovechkin has played 1,003:

894 games + 1,003 games = 1,897 games
1,897 games ÷ 2 = 948.5 games

This will be used as an estimate for the number of games McDavid will have played after thirteen seasons. From there, it is possible to project his statistics by multiplying his per-game averages by the estimated number of games he will have played.

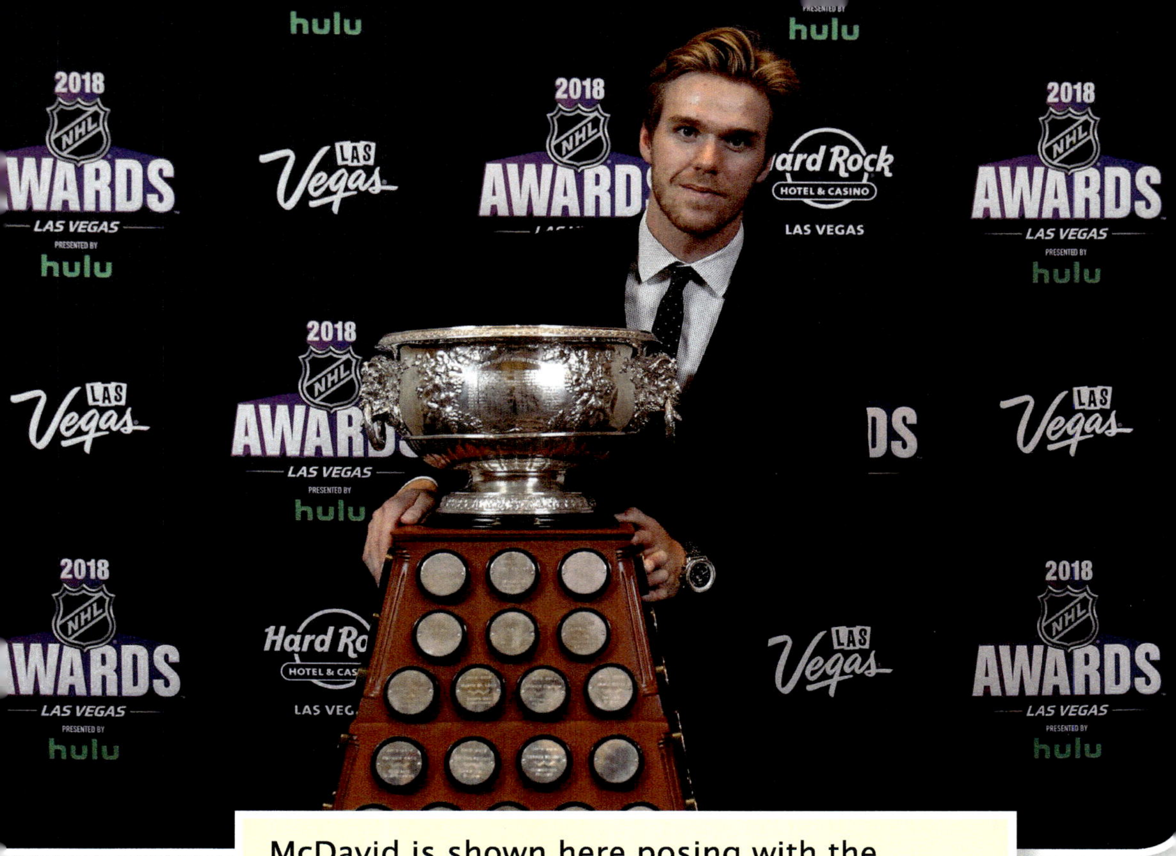

McDavid is shown here posing with the 2018 Art Ross Trophy after finishing with the most points during the regular season.

Points: 1.22 PPG × 948.5 games = 1,157 points
Goals: 0.42 GPG × 948.5 games = 398 goals
Assists: 0.81 APG × 948.5 games = 768 assists

Once again, McDavid's estimated numbers appear favorable in comparison to Ovechkin and Crosby, two of the greatest players in the twenty-first century. In fact, this places his estimated career point total after thirteen seasons above both Ovechkin's total as of the start of the 2018–2019 season—at 1,122—and Crosby's, at 1,116.

As a fledgling NHL superstar, the sky is the limit for Connor McDavid. As the new face of the league, the humble but well-spoken McDavid will continue to capture headlines as he skates his way toward the record books.

CHAPTER 5

PUTTING THE NUMBERS IN PERSPECTIVE

When looking at NHL player statistics, one thing is immediately obvious: players of past generations, such as Wayne Gretzky and Mario Lemieux, scored points at a rate much greater than the stars of today. However, it is important to consider generational differences and league evolution when analyzing the numbers, since raw statistics cannot tell the whole story.

A DIFFERENT GAME

The game of hockey is vastly different today than it was in the past, when these greats were putting up inconceivable numbers—by modern standards—in the 1980s. The NHL was not the international league it currently is, severely reducing the overall talent pool. Defensive strategies in general were not as mature, and shot blocking—a widespread and successful defensive approach used today—was nearly nonexistent. Further, the equipment itself was different: goaltender pads were smaller, heavier, and less effective. In total, the average goal in the 1980s was easier to score than it is today.

The evolution of the sport of hockey has led to considerable scoring differences between eras, and it can be difficult to put numbers from different time periods into proper context. To help, it is possible to calculate adjusted statistics, meaning statistics that have been altered to reflect how often points were being scored in general at the time. These tweaks can help put the numbers into perspective, as the value of points scored in higher-scoring eras is decreased, and the value of points scored in lower-scoring eras is increased. Wayne Gretzky first touched NHL ice in 1979, so that year will be the earliest considered for the statistical adjustments calculated here.

ERA-ADJUSTING STATISTICS

To find these adjusted stats, it is first necessary to calculate an adjustment modifier for each season. The adjustment modifier is a numerical way to compare that individual season's scoring average with the overall league-scoring average. The first step is to find what the overall league average goals per game (GPG) is. Each season's GPG between 1979 and 2018 is calculated here; sum each value and divide by the number of summed values to find the average:

7.02 + 7.68 + 8.02 + 7.72 + 7.88 + 7.78+ 7.94 + 7.34 + 7.42 + 7.48 + 7.36 + 6.92 + 6.96 + 7.26 + 6.48 + 5.98 + 6.28 + 5.84 + 5.28 + 5.26 + 5.50 + 5.52 + 5.24 + 5.30 + 5.14 + 6.16 + 5.90 + 5.56 + 5.82 + 5.68 + 5.58 + 5.46 + 5.44 + 5.48 + 5.46 + 5.42 + 5.54 + 5.94 = 240.04

240.04 ÷ 38 seasons = 6.32 overall league average GPG

Thus, 6.32 represents how many goals have been scored per game on average between 1979 and 2018. To find the adjustment modifier for each season, take the overall average league GPG (6.32), and divide it by that individual season's GPG:

Season	NHL GPG	Season GPG	Adj. modifier
1979–1980	6.32 ÷	7.02 =	0.90
1980–1981	6.32 ÷	7.68 =	0.82
1981–1982	6.32 ÷	8.02 =	0.79
...	... ...	... ...	...
2015–2016	6.32 ÷	5.42 =	1.17
2016–2017	6.32 ÷	5.54 =	1.14
2017–2018	6.32 ÷	5.94 =	1.06

Seasons with higher scoring than the overall league average have adjustment modifiers lower than 1, and those with lower scoring than the overall league average have adjustment modifier higher than 1. When a player's stats are multiplied by that season's adjustment modifier, the result will either be a lower total or a higher total, depending on the adjustment modifier.

COMPARING THE GREATS: ADJUSTED STATS

To demonstrate the stat adjustment system, Wayne Gretzky's stats will be altered. The adjustment modifier has been calculated for each season, so multiply each of his seasonal point totals by that season's adjustment modifier:

Season	Gretzky points		Adj. mod.		Gretzky adj. points
1979–1980	137	×	0.90	=	123.28
1980–1981	164	×	0.82	=	134.89
1981–1982	212	×	0.79	=	166.98
1982–1983	196	×	0.82	=	160.38
1983–1984	205	×	0.80	=	164.33
1984–1985	208	×	0.81	=	168.88
1985–1986	215	×	0.80	=	171.05
1986–1987	183	×	0.86	=	157.49
1987–1988	149	×	0.85	=	126.85
1988–1989	168	×	0.84	=	141.88
1989–1990	142	×	0.86	=	121.87
1990–1991	163	×	0.91	=	148.79
1991–1992	121	×	0.91	=	109.82
1992–1993	65	×	0.87	=	56.56

1993–1994	130	×	0.97	=	126.73
1994–1995	48	×	1.06	=	50.70
1995–1996	102	×	1.01	=	102.60
1996–1997	97	×	1.08	=	104.92
1997–1998	90	×	1.20	=	107.67
1998–1999	62	×	1.20	=	74.46
				Total adjusted points	2,520
				Games played	1,487
				Adjusted PGP	1.69

By summing each adjusted seasonal total, his total of adjusted points comes to 2,520. His adjusted total is 337 less than his original. These "lost" points are the statistical reflection of the fact that he played during one of the highest-scoring eras in NHL history. For the other potential GOATs, however, their point totals will increase by using this adjustment system.

Next, Alexander Ovechkin's seasonal stats are entered into the adjustment table:

Season	Ovechkin points		Adj. mod.		Ovechkin adj. points
2005–2006	106	×	1.03	=	108.70
2006–2007	92	×	1.07	=	98.50
2007–2008	112	×	1.14	=	127.25
2008–2009	110	×	1.09	=	119.39
2009–2010	109	×	1.11	=	121.22
2010–2011	85	×	1.13	=	96.22
2011–2012	65	×	1.16	=	75.20

2012-2013	56	×	1.16	=	65.03
2013-2014	79	×	1.15	=	91.06
2014-2015	81	×	1.16	=	93.71
2015-2016	71	×	1.17	=	82.75
2016-2017	69	×	1.14	=	78.68
2017-2018	87	×	1.06	=	92.52
				Total adjusted points	1,250
				Games played	1,003
				Adjusted PGP	1.25

Followed by Sidney Crosby:

Season	Crosby points		Adj. mod.		Crosby adj. points
2005-2006	102	×	1.03	=	104.60
2006-2007	120	×	1.07	=	128.48
2007-2008	72	×	1.14	=	81.80
2008-2009	103	×	1.09	=	111.79
2009-2010	109	×	1.11	=	121.22
2010-2011	66	×	1.13	=	74.72
2011-2012	37	×	1.16	=	42.81
2012-2013	56	×	1.16	=	65.03
2013-2014	104	×	1.15	=	119.88
2014-2015	84	×	1.16	=	97.18
2015-2016	85	×	1.17	=	99.06
2016-2017	89	×	1.14	=	101.48
2017-2018	89	×	1.06	=	94.65
				Total adjusted points	1,243
				Games played	864
				Adjusted PGP	1.44

Finally, McDavid:

SEASON	McDAVID POINTS		ADJ. MOD.		McDAVID ADJ. POINTS
2015–2016	100	×	1.17	=	55.94
2016–2017	100	×	1.14	=	114.02
2017–2018	108	×	1.06	=	114.85
				TOTAL ADJUSTED POINTS	285
				GAMES PLAYED	209
				ADJUSTED PGP	1.36

In summarizing the adjustments and comparing them to actual stats:

	GRETZKY	OVECHKIN	CROSBY	McDAVID
ACTUAL POINTS	2,857	1,122	1,116	256
ADJUSTED POINTS	2,520	1,250	1,243	285
ACTUAL PPG	1.92	1.12	1.29	1.22
ADJUSTED PPG	1.69	1.25	1.44	1.36

Analyzing the era-adjusted statistics gives another perspective to the accomplishments of these four hockey greats. While Gretzky's career total and points per game still reign supreme, the range of the numbers is much tighter. The increased point totals and PGP of each of the three modern players reflect how truly productive they have been in the league, despite playing in a different era.

THE ULTIMATE QUESTION

All things considered, who is the greatest hockey player of all time? The question means many things to many people. From those who remember the glory of Gretzky in his prime, those who were raised hearing Ovechkin ring the bell, who saw Crosby raise the Stanley Cup, or McDavid usher in a new era, each hockey fan may have his or her own answer. Whether it is points, championships, potential, or impact on the game that matters most is a decision every hockey fan makes on his or her own. The National Hockey League's record books tell the stories of the greatest hockey players ever to lace up skates. Greatness is about being remembered, and each of these hockey players will live on as some of the best ever to touch the ice.

GLOSSARY

All-Star A player selected to participate in the annual NHL All-Star Game.

Art Ross Trophy The seasonal NHL award given to the player who accumulated the most points throughout the regular season.

assist When a player aids another player who scores a goal, typically by passing him or her the puck shortly before a goal is scored; worth one point.

average Another term used for mean; the number that represents a normalized value of several other numbers.

Calder Memorial Trophy The seasonal NHL award given to the player voted to be the most outstanding rookie.

difference The value obtained by subtracting one number from another.

goal When a player shoots the puck into the opposing team's net; worth one point.

Hall of Fame A listing of the greatest and most influential hockey players, coaches, owners, and officials as voted by the NHL; also, a physical museum in Toronto, dedicated to those on the list.

Hart Memorial Trophy The seasonal NHL award given to the player voted to be the most valuable player throughout the regular season.

juniors Traditionally, the highest level of nonprofessional hockey.

Maurice "Rocket" Richard Trophy The seasonal NHL award given to the player who scores the highest number of goals throughout the regular season.

mean The value obtained by summing a numerical list and diving by the number of summed numbers; represents a statistical average.

median The value obtained by sorting a numerical list from least to greatest and selecting the middlemost number; represents a pivot point at which any number in the list is equally likely to fall above or below.

mode The value with the greatest number of occurrences in a numerical set.

National Hockey League (NHL) The professional North American ice hockey league; considered the highest-level ice hockey association in the world.

NHL draft The annual meeting by NHL teams to gain the contractual rights of unsigned, draft-eligible hockey prospects by selecting them in a structured turn-by-turn system.

point A symbolic representation of a goal or an assist, used to determine the number of goals and assists tallied by each player; in hockey statistics, both a goal and an assist are worth one point.

product The value obtained by multiplying one number by another.

quotient The value obtained by dividing one number by another.

sum The value obtained by adding one number to another.

FOR MORE INFORMATION

Canadian Hockey League (CHL)
305 Milner Avenue, Suite 201
Scarborough, ON M1B 3V4
Canada
(416) 332-9711
Website: http://www.chl.ca
Facebook: @CanadianHockeyLeague
Instagram and Twitter: @CHLHockey
The Canadian Hockey League is an organization that oversees the three major junior hockey leagues in Canada, including the Western Hockey League (WHL), Ontario Hockey League (OHL), and Quebec Major Junior Hockey League (QMJHL).

Hockey Canada
151 Canada Olympic Road SW, Suite 201
Calgary, AB T3B 6B7
Canada
(416) 548-7285
Website: https://www.hockeycanada.ca/en-ca/home
Facebook, Instagram, and Twitter: @HockeyCanada
Hockey Canada is the official governing hockey association in Canada and oversees regional and provincial associations. Information is available on finding local hockey programs in Canada as well as informational guides for the parents of youth hockey players.

Hockey Hall of Fame
30 Yonge Street
Toronto, ON M5E 1X8

Canada
(416) 360-7735
Website: http://hhof.com
Facebook and Twitter: @HockeyHallFame
Instagram: @thehockeyhalloffame
The Hockey Hall of Fame records and memorializes the achievements of prominent hockey players, coaches, owners, and officials. Educational material is available to learn more about inductees as well as plan trips to the museum in Toronto.

National Hockey League (NHL)
1185 Avenue of the Americas
New York, NY 10036
(800) 559-2333
Website: http://www.nhl.com
Facebook, Instagram, and Twitter: @NHL
The NHL is the official record house for NHL statistics, player information, team information, and award information. Biographical information is available for active and past NHL players, as well as ongoing NHL news and updates.

National Hockey League Players' Association (NHLPA)
10 Bay Street, Suite 1200
Toronto, ON M5J 2R8
Canada
(416) 313-2300
Website: http://www.nhlpa.com
Facebook, Instagram, and Twitter: @NHLPA
The NHL Players' Association is the official labor union of NHL players. On the NHLPA website, information can be

found on active and past NHL players, NHL player polls, and NHLPA community and youth outreach programs.

USA Hockey
1775 Bob Johnson Drive
Colorado Springs, CO 80906
(719) 576-8724
Website: http://www.usahockey.com
Facebook, Instagram, and Twitter: @USAhockey
USA Hockey oversees the majority of organized hockey in the United States, especially amateur and youth hockey. Its website contains educational material, training information, youth league information, parent guides, and more.

FOR FURTHER READING

Frederick, Shane. *Hockey Stats and the Stories Behind Them: What Every Fan Needs to Know*. Mankato, MN: Capstone Press, 2016.

Frederick, Shane. *Hockey: The Math of the Game*. Mankato, MN: Capstone Press, 2012.

Hetrick, Hans. *Stathead Hockey: How Data Changed the Sport*. Mankato, MN: Capstone Press, 2019.

Kortemeier, Tom. *Pro Hockey by the Numbers*. Mankato, MN: Capstone Press, 2016.

Linde, Barbara. *Ice Hockey: Science on Ice*. New York, NY: Lucent Press, 2018.

Martin, Brett. *STEM in Hockey*. Minneapolis, MN: ABDO Publishing, 2018.

Mikoley, Kate. *Hockey: Stats, Facts, and Figures*. New York, NY: Gareth Stevens Publishing, 2018.

Nagelhout, Ryan. *The Science of Hockey*. New York, NY: PowerKids Press, 2016.

Robinson, Tom. *Hockey: Math at the Rink*. Mankato, MN: The Child's World, Inc., 2019.

Simons, Rae. *Sports Math*. Broomall, PA: Mason Crest, 2014.

BIBLIOGRAPHY

Anderson, Shelly. "Crosby Sweeps NHL Major Awards; Malkin Rookie of Year in Big Night." *Pittsburgh Post-Gazette*, June 14, 2007. https://www.post-gazette.com.

Associated Press. "Sidney Crosby Injury Timeline." *USA Today*, May 2, 2017. https://www.usatoday.com.

Burnside, Scott. "Penguins, League Hit Jackpot with Lottery." ESPN, July 27, 2005. http://www.espn.com.

Canadian Press, The. "Connor McDavid Named Youngest Captain in NHL History." CBC, October 5, 2016. https://www.cbc.ca.

Crossman, Matt. "The Connor McDavid Story: How the Future of the NHL Became a (Reluctant) Star." Bleacher Report, October 9, 2015. https://bleacherreport.com.

DiFranco, Michael. "Alexander 'The Great' Ovechkin—Biography." The Hockey Writers, March 26, 2009. https://thehockeywriters.com.

DiFranco, Michael. "Sid 'The Kid' Crosby—Biography." The Hockey Writers, March 8, 2009. https://thehockeywriters.com.

Dyck, Henry. "Wayne Gretzky and Sidney Crosby: The Great One vs. the Next One." Bleacher Report, March 31, 2008. https://bleacherreport.com.

Gretzky.com. "The Legend of 99." Retrieved January 22, 2019. http://www.gretzky.com/bio.php.

Hockey Hall of Fame. "Wayne Gretzky—Biography." Hockey Hall of Fame. https://www.hhof.com.

Hockey Hall of Fame. "Wayne Gretzky—Career Statistics." Hockey Hall of Fame. http://www.legendsofhockey.net.

Kimelman, Adam. "Connor McDavid Drafted No. 1 by Edmonton Oilers." National Hockey League, June 26, 2015. https://www.nhl.com.

NHL.com. "Alex Ovechkin." NHL.com. Retrieved January 22, 2019. https://www.nhl.com/player/alex-ovechkin-8471214.

NHL.com. "Cereal to Superhero: 10 Great Gretzky Pop Culture Moments." National Hockey League, August 9, 2018. https://www.nhl.com.

NHL.com. "Connor McDavid." NHL.com. Retrieved February 1, 2019. https://www.nhl.com.

NHL.com. "Sidney Crosby." NHL.com. Retrieved February 1, 2019. https://www.nhl.com/player/sidney-crosby-8471675.

NHL.com. "Sidney Crosby Gets 12-Year Extension—but No Raise—from Penguins." National Hockey League, June 28, 2012. https://www.nhl.com.

NHL.com. "Wayne Gretzky." NHL.com. Retrieved January 25, 2019. https://www.nhl.com.

Sandler, Seth. "NFL, MLB, NHL, MLS & NBA: Which Leagues and Players Make the Most Money?" Bleacher Report, March 18, 2012. http://bleacherreport.com.

Woods, Michael. "Connor McDavid Was Born to Play Hockey." Star, March 17, 2012. https://www.thestar.com.

Zeisberger, Mike. "Crosby Says McDavid Is Best Player in NHL." National Hockey League, October 17, 2018. https://www.nhl.com.

INDEX

ABOUT THE AUTHOR

Jason Walker is a sports and statistics geek who spent his childhood weekends in an ice rink and his college weekends in a math book. After playing hockey through high school, he continued to watch his favorite sport while studying computer science and mathematics at John Jay College. His favorite rink food is nachos and his favorite NHL team is the Buffalo Sabres.

PHOTO CREDITS

Cover (top left), p. 5 Icon Sportswire/Getty Images, (top right) Patrick Smith/Getty Images, (bottom left) Brian Babineau/ National Hockey League/Getty Images, (bottom right) J Giamundo/Bruce Bennett/Getty Images; pp. 8, 12, 44 Bruce Bennett/Getty Images; p. 9 © NBC/Courtesy Everett Collection; pp. 14–15 NHL Images/Getty Images; p. 18 Scott Halleran/ Getty Images; p. 19 Jeff Vinnick/Getty Images; p. 20 Len Redkoles/National Hockey League/Getty Images; p. 23 David Becker/National Hockey League/Getty Images; p. 29 Sporting News Archive/Getty Images; p. 30 Gregory Shamus/National Hockey League/Getty Images; p. 34 Francois Laplante/ National Hockey League/Getty Images; p. 37 © AP Images; p. 39 Andy Devlin/National Hockey League/Getty Images.

Design: Brian Garvey; Editor: Siyavush Saidian; Photo Researcher: Sherri Jackson